Making Collectible Santas
and Christmas Ornaments in Wood

with Jim and Margie Maxwell

Fox Chapel Publishing
Box 7948F
Lancaster, Pennsylvania 17604

"Making Santa Collectibles and Christmas Ornaments in Wood" is first published 1993 by Fox Chapel Publishing. It contains some patterns from the author's previous book "Carving Christmas Tree Ornaments" which is now out of print.

Interior photography by Don Kaiser, Kaiser Studios, Clinton Missouri.
Cover photography by Bob Pollett, VMI Productions, Leola Pennsylvania.
Cover design and typography by Brian S. Reese.

Manufactured in the United States of America.
93 94 95 96 1 2 3 4 5 6

You may order additional copies of this book for the cover price plus $2.50 shipping. Try your bookstore first!

Fox Chapel Publishing
Book Orders
Box 7948
Lancaster, PA 17604

CONTENTS

FOREWORD

The Christmas season always finds my workshop joyously busy as I go about designing and carving new ornaments for our Christmas tree.

Our collection started with a small airplane I carved in 1979. The airplane was patterned after a toy I received for Christmas when I was a boy. As I hung the ornament on the tree, I began telling my wife about the other toys I received in Christmases past. These toys led to new ideas, and we began planning next year's ornaments.

Many Christmases later we now have over 50 handmade ornaments in our personal collection.

Many of my friends and fellow woodcarvers have found these unique ornaments to be challenging wood carving projects as well as excellent gifts and additions to their collections.

While carving these projects, keep this thought in mind: Handmade ornaments are becoming increasingly popular and these small creations of Christmas Art may become the valued collectibles of tomorrow.

JIM MAXWELL

ABOUT THIS BOOK

As you begin carving the patterns in this book, you will find that antique toys make great carving projects.

Antique toys are usually not true to scale, and often contain exaggerated or make-believe parts. These relaxed dimensions were practiced by toy companies to ensure a low cost ease of construction. This aids the carver by allowing a great deal of freedom and a chance to use one's own imagination.

The patterns are arranged according to the dates in which we carved them, not necessarily as to how difficult they may be. Some patterns, like the Teddy Bear, are very easy and will require little time, while others, like the Ford Tractor, are very challenging and my require as much as ten hours. I would suggest you begin your collection by selecting one of the easier projects.

TOOLS AND MATERIALS

To carve the projects in this book you will need some type of soft wood suitable for whittling. I would suggest Basswood, if available. Other suitable woods are: Clear White Pine, Sugar Pine, or Poplar.

A good whittling knife, plus a few basic carving tools will be needed:

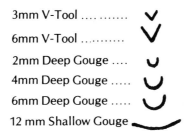

3mm V-Tool …………	V
6mm V-Tool ……….	V
2mm Deep Gouge ….	U
4mm Deep Gouge …..	U
6mm Deep Gouge …..	U
12 mm Shallow Gouge	⌣

A coping saw or band saw is used to cut out the projects.

For painting your ornaments, you will need acrylic paints and a spray can of **Deft Clear Wood Finish**.

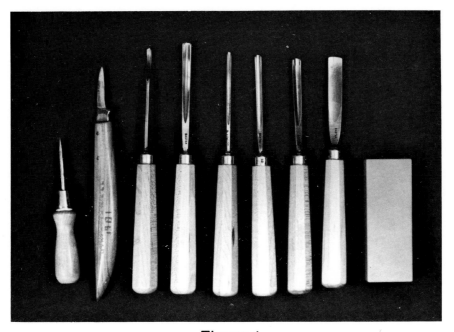

Figure 1

FINISHING

Christmas art work, for the most part, is done in bright and shiny colors. In holding with this custom, we have painted may of our ornaments in this fashion. Unlike other woodcarvings, where the artist wants a great deal of wood to show through, we prefer our Christmas ornaments to stand out against the background of a lighted tree. An occasional sparkle or highlight in the finish tends to remind us of the shiny new toys Santa leaves on Christmas morning.

Begin by sanding the ornament lightly with 220 sandpaper. Acrylic paint is then applied directly to the wood in bright colors. Sometimes lighter colors will require two coats.

Paint the smaller details on your ornaments, such as doll faces and other miniature details, which are too small to carve.

To obtain the effect of glass windows on toy vehicles, first paint the window light gray, then apply a few streaks of white, at a 45 degree angle, thus giving the illusion of light reflecting on glass.

When desired, a dark woodgrain finish can be obtained by painting an object medium brown, using burnt umber thinned with water, then streaking or woodgraining with darker burnt umber.

If you wish a natural wood finish like that used on handmade wooden toys, you need only to sand the ornament lightly and spray with clear wood finish.

After painting, we spray all our ornaments with at least three coats of Deft Clear Wood Finish. It is fast drying and will keep your ornaments clean and fresh looking for years to come.

MARGIE MAXWELL

PROCEDURES

Figure 2

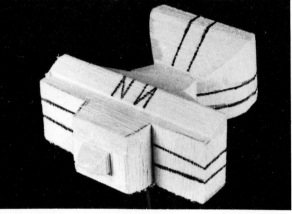

Figure 3

Figure 4

Figure 5

Figure 6

FIG. 2   DRAW OR TRACE PATTERN
ON A SOFT PIECE OF WOOD.

FIG. 3   USE A COPING OR BAND
SAW TO CUT AWAY EXTRA WOOD.

FIG. 4   BLOCK OUT ALL DIMENSIONS
WITH A KNIFE OR GOUGES.

FIG. 5   ROUND ALL CORNERS AND
EDGES TO DESIRED SHAPE.

FIG. 6   CARVE AND PAINT ON
REMAINING DETAILS.
PAINT CARVING AND SPRAY
WITH CLEAR FINISH.

Figure 7

AIRPLANE

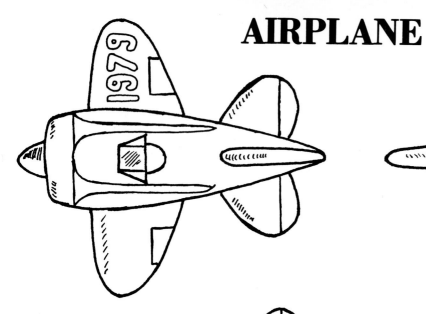

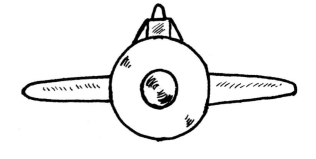

MY FIRST CHRISTMAS ORNAMENT. A SINGLE ENGINE OPEN COCKPIT MONO-WING PLANE, FINISHED IN NATURAL WOOD. DATED 1979.

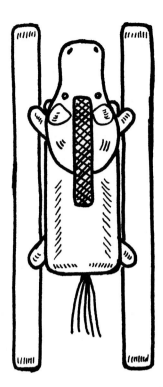

Figure 8

ROCKING HORSE

TRADITIONAL DESIGN

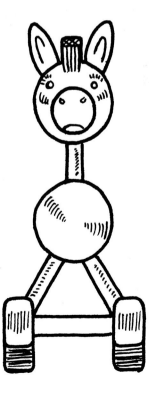

Figure 9

TRAIN ENGINE

ORIGINAL DESIGN

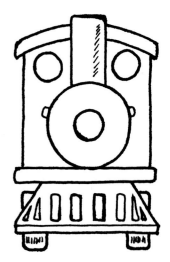

Figure 10

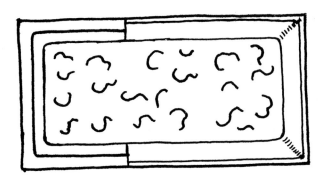

TENDER CAR

ADD ONE CAR EACH YEAR. EXTRA
PATTERNS INCLUDED FOR FREIGHT TRAIN.

Figure 11

PASSENGER CAR AND GONDOLA

PINE WOOD RAIL ROAD

TANKER, BOX CAR AND CABOOSE

Figure 12

TOY TRUCKS ARE THE MOST POPULAR OF ALL CHRISTMAS TOYS.
I ESPECIALLY LIKE THE ONES THAT HAUL LUMBER AND LOGS.

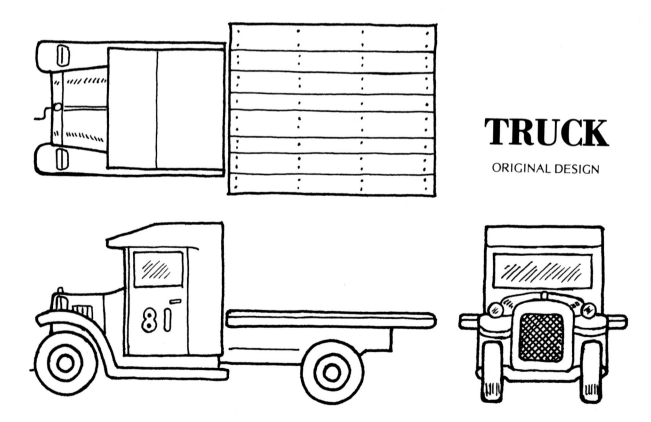

TRUCK

ORIGINAL DESIGN

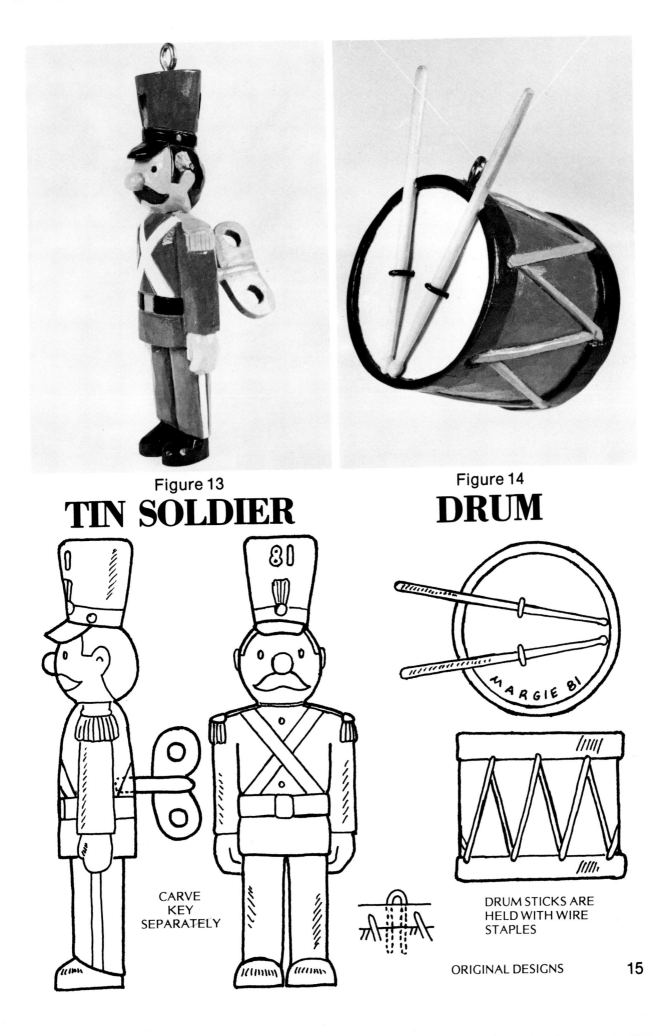

Figure 13

TIN SOLDIER

Figure 14

DRUM

CARVE
KEY
SEPARATELY

MARGIE 81

DRUM STICKS ARE
HELD WITH WIRE
STAPLES

ORIGINAL DESIGNS

15

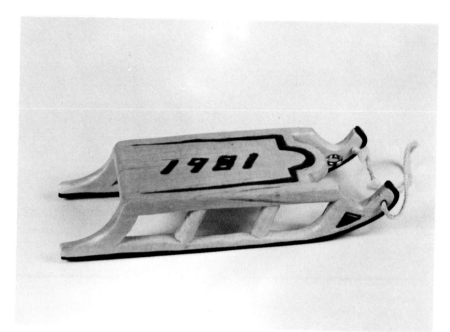

Figure 15

SLED

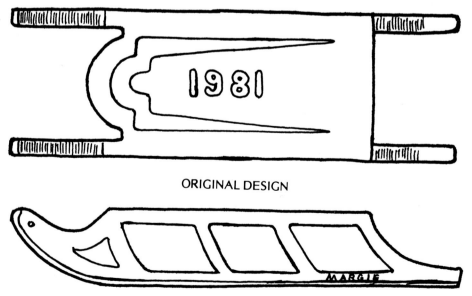

ORIGINAL DESIGN

CHRISTMAS STOCKING

Figure 16

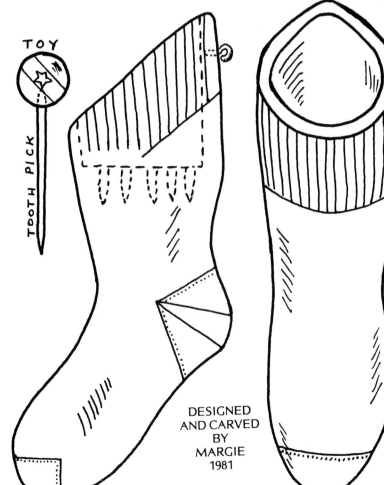

TOY

TOOTH PICK

DESIGNED
AND CARVED
BY
MARGIE
1981

TEDDY BEAR

HAIR TECHNIQUE
IS APPLIED WITH
3MM V TOOL

Figure 17

ORIGINAL DESIGN

Figure 18

DOLL BUGGY

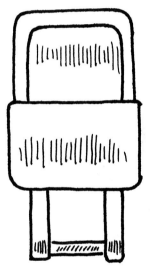

ORIGINAL DESIGN

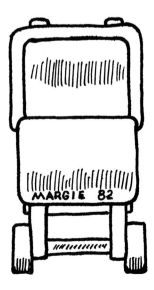

Figure 19

PATTERNED AFTER AN ARCADE TOY COMPANY CAST IRON TOY,
CIRCA 1930'S, CARVED 1983.

FORDSON TRACTOR

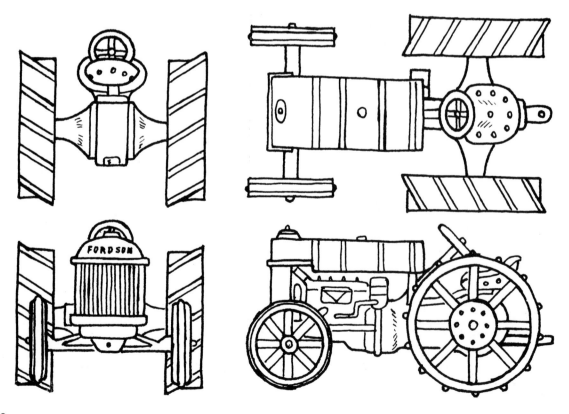

Figure 20

Figure 21

DOLL HOUSE

MARGIE   CARVED 1983
ORIGINAL DESIGN

JACK
IN THE
BOX

ORIGINAL DESIGN
CARVED 1983

Figure 22

Figure 23

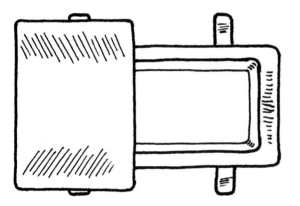

DOLL CRADLE

ORIGINAL DESIGN

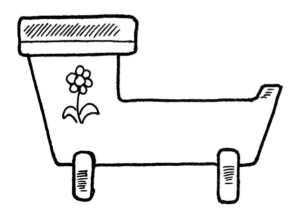

Figure 24

STEAM SHOVEL

ORIGINAL DESIGN

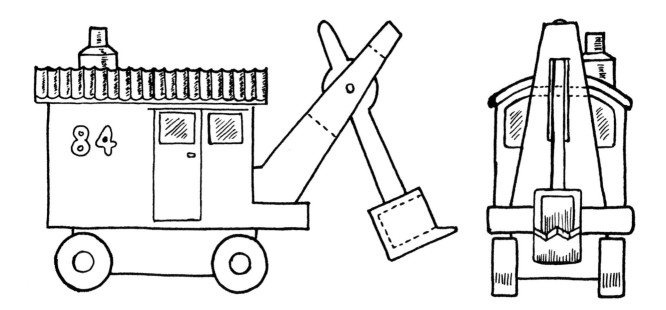

VILLAGE CHURCH

CARVED BY MARGIE

ONE OF TODAY'S FASTEST GROWING CHRISTMAS COLLECTIBLES IS SMALL VILLAGE BUILDINGS, WE ADD TWO BUILDINGS EACH YEAR TO OUR COLLECTION WHICH BEGAN WITH THIS SMALL CHURCH. WE NOW HAVE A SMALL TOWN COMPLETE WITH A LIKENESS OF OUR OWN WOOD CARVING SHOP.

SNOW MAN

WINTER SNOW IS CONSIDERED BY MANY TO BE THE BEST PART OF CHRISTMAS. I LOVE MAKING THE LARGE SNOW SCULPTURES AT CHRISTMAS TIME. BUT WHEN NO SNOW IS AVAILABLE I ALSO ENJOY CARVING SMALL ONES OUT OF WOOD.

THE PIPE IS MADE SEPARATELY AND INSTALLED LAST.

Figure 26

GRAF ZEPPELIN

PATTERNED AFTER A STEELCRAFT TOY 1930'S

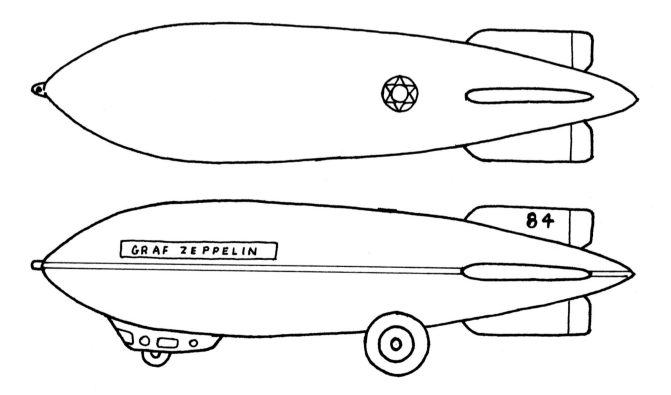

RAG DOLL

TRADITIONAL DESIGN

Figure 27

MARGIE MAXWELL 84

27

Figure 25

TUG BOAT

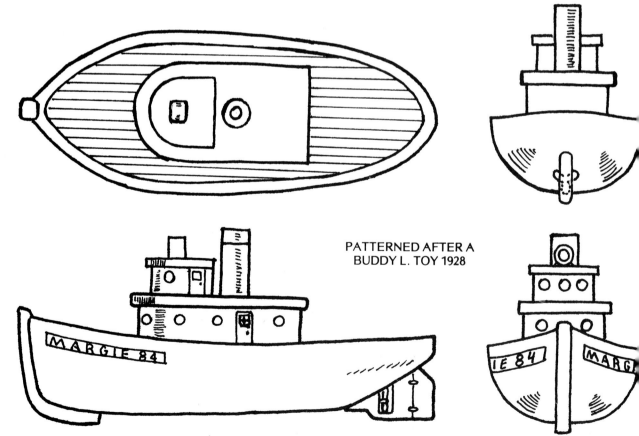

PATTERNED AFTER A
BUDDY L. TOY 1928

MARGIE 84

ANTIQUE SANTA COLLECTION

TH THE INCREASING POPULARITY OF COLLECTING
RISTMAS ORNAMENTS, OLD SANTAS HAVE BECOME
E MOST DESIRABLE AND HARDEST TO OBTAIN.

RE ARE SOME OF OUR FAVORITE PATTERNS FOR OLD
D RARE SANTAS WHICH WE HAVE CARVED FOR OUR
DLLECTION.

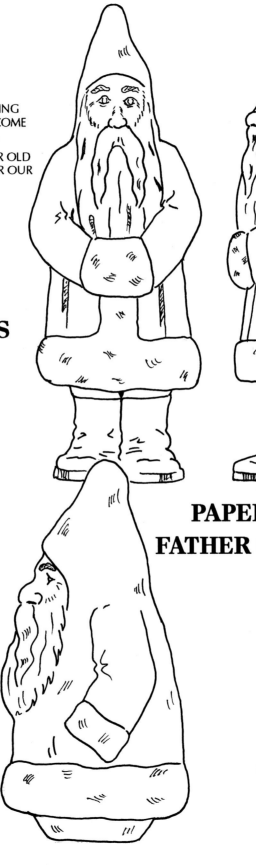

CAST IRON
FATHER CHRISTMAS

CIRCA 1905

PAPER-MACHE
FATHER CHRISTMAS

CIRCA 1920

GLASS SANTA FACE

CIRCA 1930

OLD GLASS ORNAMENTS HAVE NO SHA[RP]
EDGES. ALL DETAIL SHOULD BE SMOOTH
AND SLIGHTLY ROUNDED. THE BEARD IS
FORMED BY MAKING SHALLOW CUTS W[ITH]
A 4MM GOUGE. SAND LIGHTLY WITH VE[RY]
FINE SAND PAPER.

FOLK ART
FATHER CHRISTMAS

THERE ARE MANY DIFFERENT VERSIONS OF THIS FIGURE
RANGING FROM VERY CRUDE TO SOME THAT LOOK
VERY PROFESSIONAL.

SOME VERSIONS FEATURE SANTA HOLDING CHRISTMAS
TREES AND/OR TOYS.

THIS FIGURE WAS CARVED BY MARGIE. SHE PAINTS
THEM IN A VARIETY OF OLD WORLD COLORS.

30

ROLY POLY SANTA

CIRCA 1920

ORIGINALLY MADE OF LITHOGRAPHED TIN, THESE HAPPY LITTLE SANTAS WOULD UPRIGHT THEMSELVES WHEN TIPPED OVER. DETAILS SHOULD BE CARVED VERY SHALLOW TO CREATE THE LOOK OF PAINTED TIN.

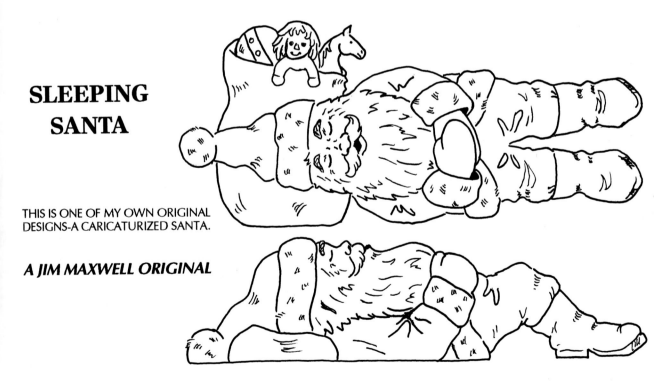

SLEEPING SANTA

THIS IS ONE OF MY OWN ORIGINAL DESIGNS-A CARICATURIZED SANTA.

A JIM MAXWELL ORIGINAL

"SLEEPING SANTA" IS ONE OF MY PERSONAL FAVORITES. A NICE PROJECT FOR THE CARVER WHO WANTS AN ADVANCED PROJECT.

SANTA

Figure 28

ORIGINAL
DESIGN
1984

For additional instructions — refer to
CARVING CARICATURES FROM THE MISSOURI
FOOTHILLS by Jim Maxwell © 1982

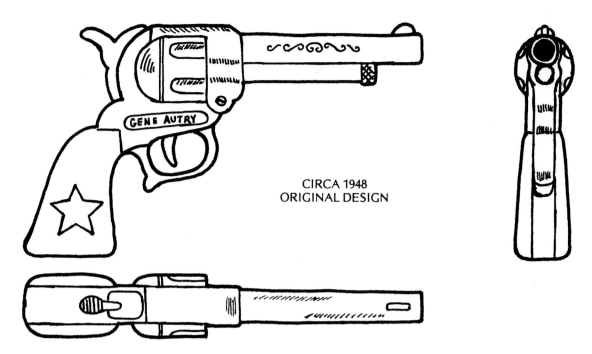

CIRCA 1948
ORIGINAL DESIGN

GENE AUTRY CAP PISTOL

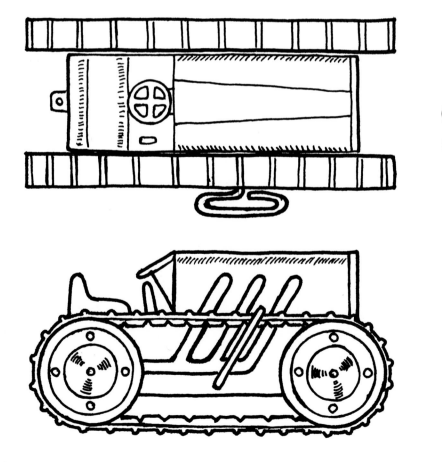

MIGHTY CLIMBING TRACTOR

KEY WIND
LITHOGRAPH TIN
CIRCA 1938

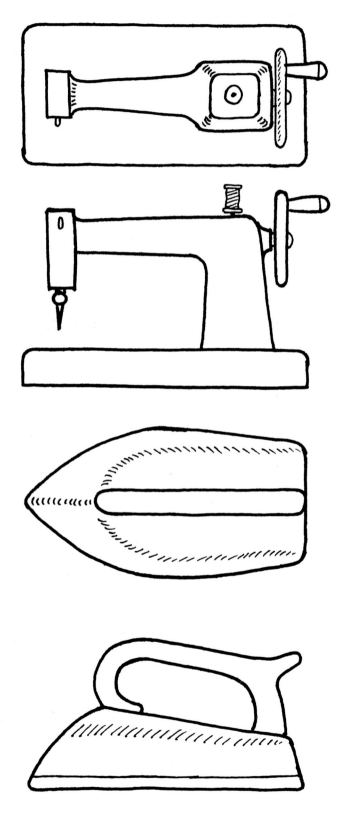

SEWING MACHINE

CIRCA 1955

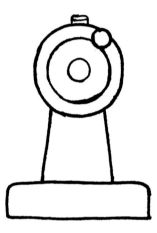

IRON

CIRCA 1950

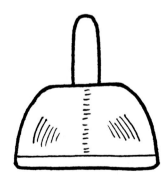

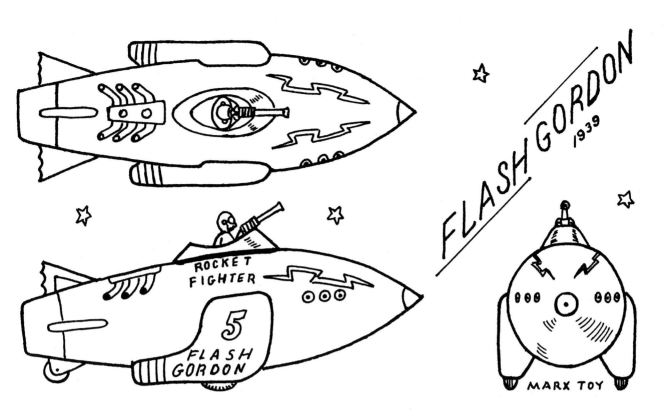

SPACE TOYS OF YESTERDAY

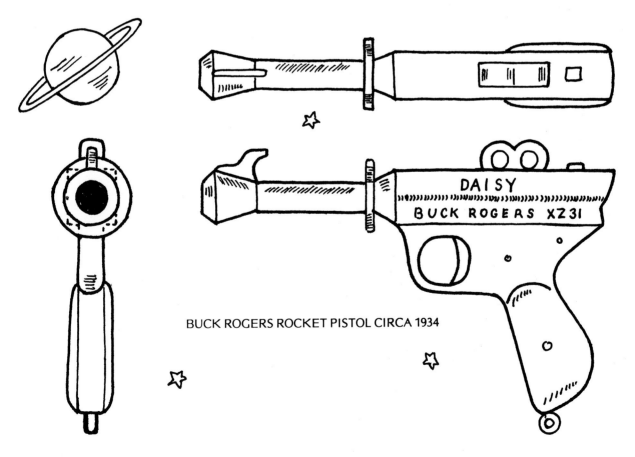

BUCK ROGERS ROCKET PISTOL CIRCA 1934

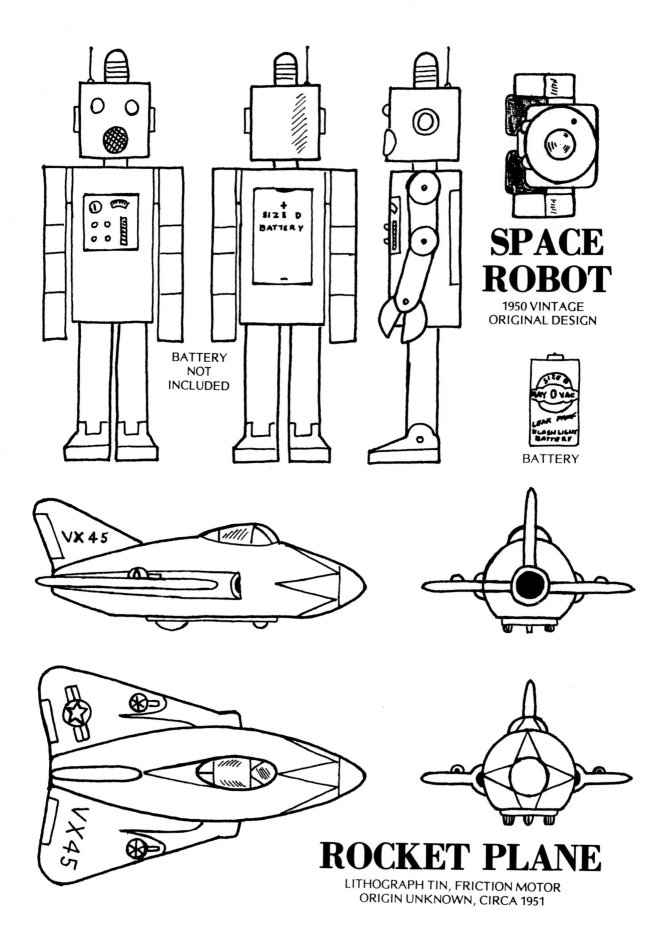

BATTERY
NOT
INCLUDED

SPACE
ROBOT

1950 VINTAGE
ORIGINAL DESIGN

BATTERY

ROCKET PLANE

LITHOGRAPH TIN, FRICTION MOTOR
ORIGIN UNKNOWN, CIRCA 1951

Encyclopedia of Bird Reference Drawings
by David Mohrhardt

"I feel this book will become the one most frequently opened in your studio. You will find it unique in that it offers information not always provided in other reference books". -Bob Guge

This re-issue classic features detailed sketches and wing studies for more than 215 different birds. Includes lots of hard to find information. David is an award winning artist, has been featured at the Leigh Yawkey Woodsom Museum and has a real gift for teaching. We recommend this book as an excellent general reference. Great buy for all carvers, bird lovers and artists.
1-56523-009-4 $14.95

Carving Books by Ivan Whillock

Ivan Whillock is a creative master woodcarver. His books are easy to follow with clear directions and excellent step-by-step photographs and sketches.
Pictorial Relief Carving- projects and patterns
17 projects many photos
Whill2 $9.95
Head Proportions Made Simple
This book will be of real help in understanding what you need to carve faces and figures.
Whill1 $6.00
Carving the Head in Wood- Step-by-step Instruction.
Good clear instructions with over 200 photos cover all aspects from start to finish.
Whill3 $14.95

Carving Characters with Jim Maxwell

New printing of this popular book! Jim has included twelve of his all-time favorite patterns drawn from childhood memories. These projects are designed to be easy to carve whether you are a beginner or advanced carver. These projects feature step-by-step photos and instructions making it easy to quickly understand Jim's techniques and procedures. Want to carve characters? This book takes you from start to finish.
 # Maxwell1   only $6.95

Making Collectible Santas and Christmas Ornaments in Wood.

These 42 easy-to-follow projects will make you very popular this Christmas! Great items for money-making sales as well. This wonderful book presents a variety of projects from traditional to modern, including Santa Clauses and replicas of antique toy ornaments.
Jim and his wife Margie have been making unique carved Santas and wooden Christmas ornaments for over a decade. This new book replaces their earlier book "Carving Christmas Tree Ornaments" and offers eight new, never-before-published patterns for you to make. Highly recommended and a great value.
#Maxwell2   only $6.95

Mammals - An Artistic Approach

Desiree Hajny- to publish first book in Fall 1993.
Nebraska carver Desiree Hajny, well known for her carving seminars and beautiful carved animals will be sharing her knowledge and carving secrets in a new book to be published this fall. Tentatively titled "Mammals: An Artistic Approach" it will be both an excellent reference work on anatomy as well as a complete step-by-step technique book with detailed patterns. This book will start out by teaching you all about mammal anatomy and movement. Then Desiree walks you through some projects step-by-step so you can pick up her tips and techniques in an easy, natural way. Use the patterns to start your own projects then finish it off using Desiree's hair tract burning patterns and painting directions.
Patterns Included: Deer and Fawn, River Otters, Black Bear + more.
Mammals: An Artistic Approach (Hajny 1) $19.95

WOODCARVER'S WORKBOOK

Best woodcarving pattern book I have seen in my 40 years as a carver!
Ed Gallenstein, President
National Woodcarvers Association
Through her articles in Chip Chats-the National Wood Carvers Association magazine- Master artist Mary Duke Guldan has helped thousands of carvers develop their carving skills.
Follow these complete step-by-step instructions and easy to follow patterns-soon you will be creating beautiful hand carved pieces of your own. A special section on painting and finishing your heirloom carving is found in the back of the book.
Look inside and see for yourself why this book is considered a classic by both beginner and veteran carvers.
This excellent woodcarving manual features patterns for : Cougar, Rabbit, Wolf Dogs, Whitetail Deer, Bighorn Sheep,Wild Mustang Horse,Unicorn, Moose
Woodcarvers Workbook (guldan) $14.95

Second Woodcarvers Workbook

All-new patterns, projects and techniques from your favorite carving author. This new book will contain more than just animals. Partial Listing of Pattern Contents Texas Longhorn, Cows, Bulls and Farm Animals
Native Indian Chief, Elk, Bears
Second Woodcarvers Workbook Fall 1993 (guldan2) $14.95

Carving Wooden Critters
by Diane Ernst

Curious bunnies, playful puppies-the projects in this book are cute! Delightful patterns at a great price! This inexpensive book features more than a dozen great projects. Easy to follow, clear patterns. Step-by-step beginners' section in front. Great gift and sale items ideas.
(Ernst1) only $6.95

Take a Look at Our Other Fine Woodworking Books

Woodcarving Books by George Lehman

Learn new techniques as you carve these projects designed by professional artists and carver George Lehman. These best-selling books by a master carver are invaluable reference books, PLUS each book contains over 20 ready-to-use patterns.

Book One - Carving Realistic Game and Songbirds - Patterns and instructions

Enthusiastically received by carvers across the US and Canada. George pays particular attention to the needs of beginning carvers in this volume. 20 patterns, over 70 photos, sketches and reference drawing.
ISBN# 1-56523-004-3   96 pages, spiral bound, 14 x 11 inches, includes index, resources $19.95

Book Two - Realism in Wood - 22 projects, detailed patterns and instructions

This volume features a selection of patterns for shorebirds and birds of prey in addition to all-new duck and songbird patterns. Special sections on adding detail, burning.
ISBN# 1-56523-005-1.   112 pages, spiral bound, 14 x 11 inches, includes index, resources $19.95

Book Three - Nature in Wood - patterns for carving 21 smaller birds and 8 wild animals

Focuses on songbirds and small game birds . Numerous tips and techniques throughout including instruction on necessary skills for creating downy feather details and realistic wings. Wonderful section on wild animal carvings with measured patterns.
ISBN #1-56523-006-X   128 pages, soft bound, 11 x 8.5 inches, includes index, resources $16.95

Book Four - Carving Wildlife in Wood- 20 Exciting Projects

Here is George's newest book for decorative woodcarvers with never-before-published patterns. Tremendously detailed, these patterns appeal to carvers at all skill levels. Patterns for birds of prey, ducks, wild turkey, shorebirds and more! Great addition to any carvers library - will be used again and again.
ISBN #1-56523-007-8   96 pages, spiral-bound, 14 x 11 inches, includes index, resources $19.95

Easy to Make Wooden Inlay Projects: Intarsia   by Judy Gale Roberts

Intarsia is a method of making picture mosaics in wood, using a combination of wood grains and colors. The techniques and step-by-step instructions in this book will have you completing your own beautiful pieces in short order. Written by acknowledged expert Judy Gale Roberts, who has her own studio and publishes the Intarsia Times newsletter, produces videos, gives seminars and writes articles on the Intarsia method. Each project is featured in full color and this well written, heavily illustrated features over 100 photographs and includes index and directory of suppliers
ISBN# 56523-023-X   250 pages, soft cover, 8.5 x 11 inches $19.95

Two more great scroll saw books by Judy Gale Roberts! Scroll Saw Fretwork Patterns

Especially designed for the scroll saw enthusiast who wishes to excel, the 'fine line design' method helps you to control drift error found with thick line patterns. Each book features great designs, expert tips, and patterns on oversized (up to 11" x 17" !) sheets in a special "lay flat" spiral binding. Choose the original Design Book 1 with animal and fun designs, or Design Book Two featuring "Western- Southwestern" designs.
Scroll Saw Fretwork Pattern, Design Book One "The Original" $14.95
Scroll Saw Fretwork Patterns, Design Book Two "Western-Southwestern" $16.95

Scroll Saw Woodcrafting Magic! Complete Pattern and How-to Manual   by Joanne Lockwood

Includes complete patterns drawn to scale. You will be amazed at how easy it is to make these beautiful projects when you follow Joanne's helpful tips and work from these clear, precise patterns. Never-before-published patterns for original and creative toys, jewelry, and gifts. Never used a scroll saw? The tutorials in this book will get you started quickly. Experienced scroll-sawers will delight in these all-new, unique projects, perfect for craft sales and gift-giving. Written by Joanne Lockwood, owner of Three Bears Studio in California and the president of the Sacramento Area Woodworkers; she is frequently featured in national woodwork and craft magazines.
ISBN# 1-56523-024-8   180 pages, soft cover, 8.5 x 11 inches $14.95

Making Signs in Wood with Your Router   by Paul Merrills

If you own a router, you can produce beautiful personalized signs and designs easily and inexpensively. This is the complete manual for beginners and professionals. Features over 100 clear photos, easy-to-follow instructions, ready-to-use designs, and six complete sign making alphabets. Techniques range from small nameplates to world-class showpieces trimmed with gold leaf.
ISBN# 56523-026-4 250 pages, 8.5 x 11 inches; includes index and suppliers directory $19.95

- -

To order: If you can't find these at your favorite bookseller you may order direct from the publisher at the prices listed above plus $2.00 per book shipping.
Send check or money order to:

Fox Chapel Publishing
Box 7948D
Lancaster, Pennsylvania , 17604